FOLK HEROES

Paul Revere

LILY ERLIC

MEDIA ENHANCED BOOKS
AV2 BY WEIGL
ADDED VALUE • AUDIO VISUAL
www.av2books.com

Published by AV² by Weigl
350 5th Avenue, 59th Floor
New York, NY 10118
Website: www.av2books.com

Library of Congress Cataloging-in-Publication Data
Names: Erlic, Lily, author.
Title: Paul Revere / Lily Erlic.
Description: New York, NY : AV2 by Weigl, [2020] | Series: Folk heroes | Audience: Ages 9. | Audience: Grades 4-6. | Includes index.
Identifiers: LCCN 2019006894 (print) | LCCN 2019010677 (ebook) | ISBN 9781489695529 (multi User ebook) | ISBN 9781489695536 (single User ebook) | ISBN 9781489695505 (hardcover :alk. paper) | ISBN 9781489695512(softcover :alk. paper)
Subjects: LCSH: Revere, Paul, 1735-1818--Juvenile literature. | Statesmen--Massachusetts--Biography--Juvenile literature. | United States--History--Revolution, 1775-1783--Biography--Juvenile literature.
Classification: LCC F69.R43 (ebook) | LCC F69.R43 E75 2020 (print) | DDC 973.3/311092 [B] --dc23
LC record available at https://lccn.loc.gov/2019006894

Printed in Guangzhou, China
1 2 3 4 5 6 7 8 9 0 23 22 21 20 19

042019
311018

Project Coordinator: Heather Kissock
Art Director: Terry Paulhus

Photo Credits
Weigl acknowledges Getty Images and Alamy as its primary image suppliers for this title.

Paul Revere

CONTENTS

A True Patriot

Paul Revere was a folk hero of the **War of Independence**. He is best known for a horseback ride he took late one night. Paul rode to warn **Patriot** leaders that British soldiers were on their way. The story of his ride was told in a poem. The poem made Paul famous across the land.

Paul helped the Patriots in other ways, too. As an **activist**, he was not afraid to stand up for his beliefs. He fought against British taxes. He also helped **colonists** stay safe from the British army.

"...I was one of upwards of 30...who formed...a committee for the purpose of watching the movements of the British soldiers..."

– Paul Revere

At the time of his ride, Paul was a successful businessman. He owned a shop that made metal goods.

More than 13,000 people lived in Boston by the time Paul was born.

Growing Up

Paul Revere was born on January 1, 1735, in Boston, Massachusetts. He was one of 12 children. Paul's father, Apollos, worked as a **silversmith**. His mother, Deborah, took care of the family.

Paul attended school until he was 13 years old. By then, he had the writing, reading, and math skills he needed to become a silversmith. Paul began working in his father's shop. He was talented and learned quickly. It was not long before Paul became a **master craftsman**.

As a teenager, Paul worked as a bell ringer at his local church.

Paul's Protest

When Paul was 19 years old, his father passed away. Paul took over his father's business. He made tea sets, medical tools, pots, and **flatware** for the people of Boston. Many of the city's richest people had his silver in their homes.

Paul became worried about the way the British were taxing businesses. In 1773, he joined a group called the Sons of Liberty. Here, he met people who were planning to **protest** the taxes. Paul decided to protest, too. One night, Paul and the other men climbed onto three British boats. The boats had boxes of tea on board. The men threw the tea into the water. This protest is now known as the Boston Tea Party.

Paul helped throw 90,000 pounds (40,823 kilograms) of tea into Boston Harbor. That much tea would be worth almost $1 million today.

Many of the men who took part in the Boston Tea Party dressed as Native Americans. This was so that no one would know who they were.

As he rode to Lexington, Paul warned colonists that the British were coming their way.

Ride to Lexington

Paul was a good horseback rider. He could ride quickly when needed. Paul worked as a **courier** for the Boston Committee of Safety. This group acted as the Patriot government in Boston. On April 18, 1775, the committee asked Paul to ride to the town of Lexington. He was to warn Patriot leaders that the British were coming to capture them.

Paul borrowed a horse from a friend. He then began the ride to Lexington. British soldiers tried to stop him, but Paul escaped. He made it to Lexington in time to warn the leaders. Paul tried to go to Concord as well, but was captured by the British. He was let go after a few hours.

"The **regulars** are coming out!"

– Paul Revere, upon arriving in Lexington

The Look of a Legend

Paul Revere was 40 years old when he took his famous ride. The clothes he wore during his ride were likely typical Patriot attire. Paul would have looked like most other colonists in the area.

Paintings of Paul's ride often show him wearing a heavy overcoat. As the ride took place on a cold night, the coat would have given him extra warmth.

Think About It

People's clothing can say a great deal about them. What do Paul's clothes say about him? Why did he dress like other colonists? What were the advantages of doing this? If it was a cold night and you had to go on Paul Revere's ride, what clothing would you wear? Think about how important his clothes were to him on the ride.

Tricornes were popular during the time of Paul's ride. These hats were called tricornes because they had three corners.

Knee breeches were common during colonial times. Everyday breeches were usually made of leather or wool. They came down to the knee where they were fastened with a buckle.

While most Patriots wore leather shoes for footwear, Paul may have worn high-topped riding boots during his ride. Made of leather, they are designed to protect the rider's legs.

About 75 colonists took part in the Battle of Lexington on April 19, 1775. They fought about 700 British soldiers.

A Helping Hand

The War of Independence began in Lexington the day after Paul's ride. Paul's warning had helped the Patriots prepare for the British attack. Paul continued to help the Patriot cause during the war. He made gunpowder for the Patriots. He also became the commander of a fort in Boston Harbor.

After the war, Paul returned to business. He opened a copper mill. It was the first mill of its kind in the United States. Paul also opened a hardware store and a **foundry**. Paul died in 1818, at the age of 83.

Paul's company, Revere Copper Products, opened in 1801 and is still operating today.

Paul Today

For a long time, very few people knew the story of Paul and his ride. This changed in 1861. That year, a poem about Paul appeared in a magazine. The poem was written by a man named Henry Wadsworth Longfellow. It was called *Paul Revere's Ride*. People all over America read about Paul and his ride. The poem made Paul a folk hero.

Today, people can visit the Paul Revere House in Boston. This is where Paul lived with his family. Visitors can see furniture that once belonged to Paul. Some of Paul's silverwork is also on display.

"So through the night rode Paul Revere
And so through the night went his cry of alarm"

– Henry Wadsworth Longfellow,
Paul Revere's Ride

The Boston house was built in 1680. Paul owned it from 1770 to 1800.

Timeline of Paul Revere

1735
Paul Revere is born on January 1, in Boston, Massachusetts.

1748
Paul begins working at his father's business.

1754
Paul's father dies. Paul takes over the family business.

1757
Paul marries Sarah Orne. They go on to have eight children.

1770
Paul buys a house in Boston's North End.

1773
Sarah dies, and Paul marries Rachel Walker. They have eight children together.

Paul Revere was one of many colonists who questioned British rule. He took an active role in fighting for colonists' rights. His ride to warn Patriot leaders of a British attack became known throughout the land. The story of this ride made Paul the folk hero he is today.

1774
Paul joins a Patriot spy ring called "The Mechanics."

1801
Paul opens a copper mill.

1818
Paul dies at the age of 83.

1775
Paul rides to Lexington to warn the Patriots that the British are coming.

What Have You Learned?

Test your knowledge of Paul Revere by answering the following questions.

1

True or False?
Paul was born in Massachusetts.

2

What type of hat did Paul wear?

a) Tricorne
b) Nightcap
c) Top hat
d) Baseball cap

3

How old was Paul when he took his famous ride?

a) 35
b) 37
c) 40
d) 42

4

True or False?
Paul had 16 children.

5

True or False?

Paul rode his father's horse on his ride to Lexington.

6

True or False?

The War of Independence started on the day Paul took his ride.

7

When did Paul join the Sons of Liberty?

a) 1773
b) 1775
c) 1780
d) 1781

8

True or False?

Henry Wadsworth Longfellow wrote a poem about Paul Revere.

9

True or False?

Paul was captured by the British before he reached Lexington.

10

True or False?

Paul wore an overcoat when he rode to Lexington.

ANSWERS

1 True 2 a) 3 c) 4 True 5 False. He rode a friend's horse. 6 False. The war started the day after Paul's ride. 7 a) 8 True 9 False. Paul reached Lexington, but was captured before he could get to Concord. 10 True

Two Sides to a Story

To Americans, Paul Revere was a hero. The British, however, did not see Paul in the same light. To them, he was a problem.

Use the library and the internet to research Paul Revere. Draw a line down the middle of a piece of paper. Label one side "Colonists" and the other side "British." Write out your notes on the paper as you research. Try to answer the following questions.

1. What qualities or events make Paul a hero?
2. How could these qualities or events make him a problem for the British?

When your research is complete, read your notes. Do you think Paul was a hero or a problem? Why?

Key Words

activist: a person who fights for what he or she believes in

colonists: people who live in a land ruled by another nation

courier: a person who delivers items to other people

flatware: eating and serving utensils, such as knives and forks

foundry: a place where metals are cast into shapes and forms

master craftsman: a worker who practices a trade or handicraft with a high degree of skill

Patriot: a person who sided with the colonies during the War of Independence

protest: to take action against something that is wrong or unfair

regulars: British soldiers

silversmith: a person who makes items from silver

War of Independence: the fight that Americans waged to become free from British rule

Index

Log on to www.av2books.com

AV^2 by Weigl brings you media enhanced books that support active learning. Go to www.av2books.com, and enter the special code found on page 2 of this book. You will gain access to enriched and enhanced content that supplements and complements this book. Content includes video, audio, weblinks, quizzes, a slideshow, and activities.

AV^2 Online Navigation

Book Pages
AV^2 pages directly correspond to pages in the book.

Audio
Listen to sections of the book read aloud.

Video
Watch informative video clips.

Embedded Weblinks
Gain additional information for research.

Key Words
Study vocabulary, and complete a matching word activity.

Try This!
Complete activities and hands-on experiments.

Quizzes
Test your knowledge.

Slideshow
View images and captions, and prepare a presentation.

AV^2 was built to bridge the gap between print and digital. We encourage you to tell us what you like and what you want to see in the future.

Sign up to be an AV^2 Ambassador at www.av2books.com/ambassador.

Due to the dynamic nature of the internet, some of the URLs and activities provided as part of AV^2 by Weigl may have changed or ceased to exist. AV^2 by Weigl accepts no responsibility for any such changes. All media enhanced books are regularly monitored to update addresses and sites in a timely manner. Contact AV^2 by Weigl at 1-866-649-3445 or av2books@weigl.com with any questions, comments, or feedback.